Meet Ian, the Hurricane

Pat Goldys

https://voadflorida.wpengine.com/

Dedicated to all the victims of Hurricane Ian. Prayers and support for Florida.

To all the neighborhoods that helped each other through this scary time. Gratitude to all who came to the rescue during hurricanes!

Thanks to my granddaughter, Mila, who did weather reports on facebook for our family and friends in Baltimore.

Thank you to Iralia and Judy, who contributed photos.
Thanks to the contributions of the Venetian Bay community for their photos: Candace McKinley, Donna Rechichar, Jim Powers, Tamara Phipps, Randolph Brands, Scott Fogle, Malisa Kurtz, Donna Wyborgny, Beth Polk Grantham, Jana Lanier, Karen Tosoni, Lydia Dawn, Jessica Fitzgerald, JoAnn Annett
Thank you!

The weather person said a hurricane was coming our way. We were told to prepare for its arrival on Wednesday at 3:00 am.

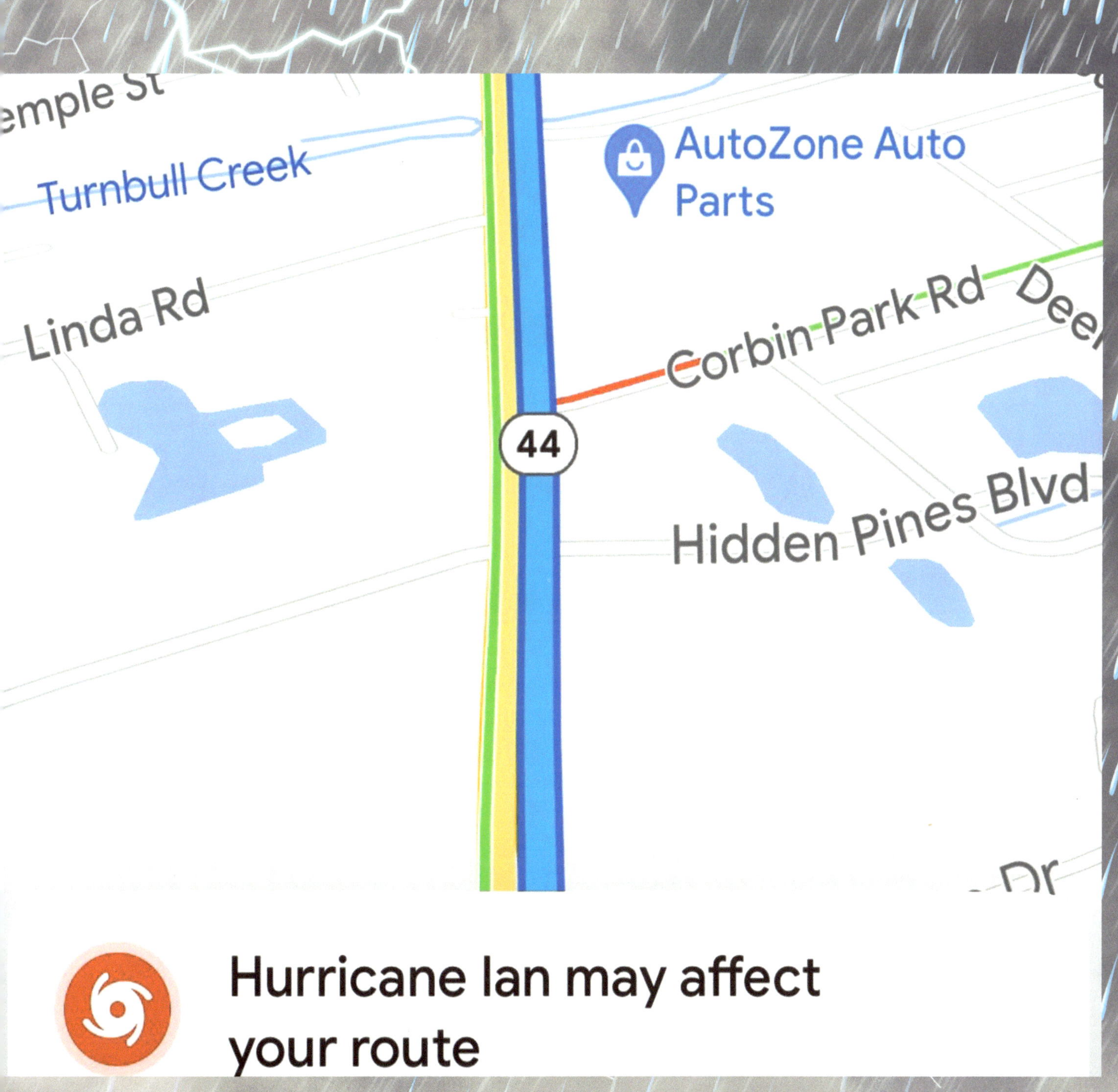
emple St
Turnbull Creek
Linda Rd
AutoZone Auto
Parts
Corbin Park Rd
Deer
44
Hidden Pines Blvd
Dr
Hurricane Ian may affect
your route

All the neighbors prepared by getting together their hurricane survival kits. Grandma's kit had flashlight and batteries, first aid kit, bottles of water, food that didn't need refrigeration, propane and a generator for electricity. When the power goes out, a generator will keep the refrigerator cold, phones charged, and fan running.

Everything that was on the floor in the house was picked up, so if water got in, nothing would get wet. Grandpa hung the hurricane shutters on the windows.

When the hurricane arrived, the wind was blowing and rain pouring. Grandma and grandpa were safe and dry in bed. Over 19 inches of rain took over the community.

The next day, there was no power. The streets were filled with water. It looked like a river running past her home. No television, no air conditioning, no cooking and no light. So, candles were lit and flashlights were used to see in places that were dark in the house.

Pollela Ave
Stefano St

Finally, the rain stopped. The sun came out. The neighbors came out of their homes to see if there was any damage. Stores were closed due to power outages.

Did sand bags keep water from coming in house or garage?

CLOSED
For the safety of
our guests we will
be closed until the
storm passes and
power is ensured.

Some cars were stuck in the flood waters. The water was up to an adult's knees. People were told not to walk in the dirty water. It was hard not to splash in the water. Water was everywhere and people wanted to see their neighborhood after the storm. Some people kayaked, paddle boarded, surfed and bicycled in the flood to have some fun after being in the house for so long.

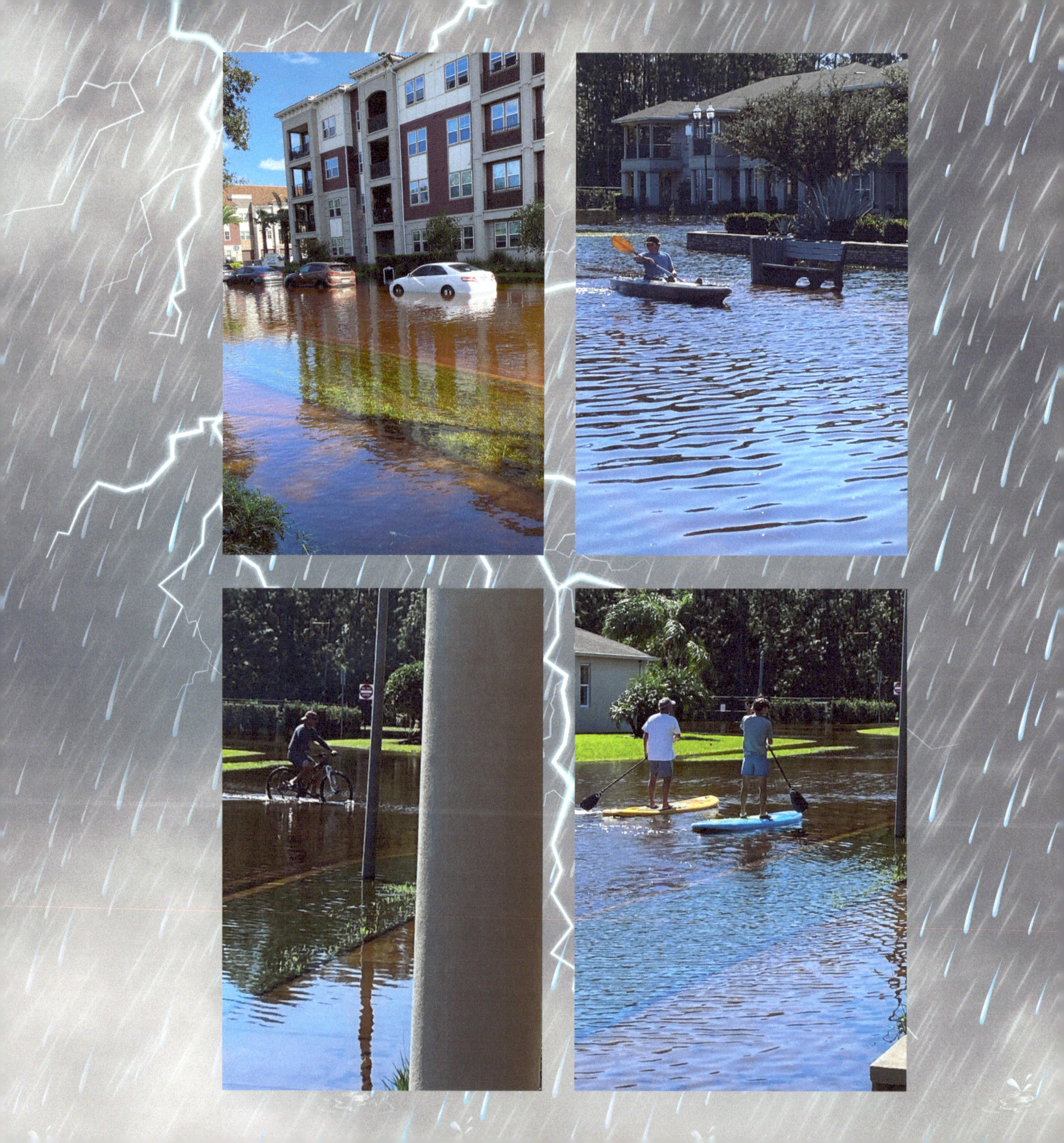

Things do get damaged in a hurricane. Trees fall, debris scattered about, cars stuck, windows broken, and insides flooded with rain water. Signs are blown down. People are rescued from their homes and taken to shelters. Some evacuate before the storm because they are in a flood zone.

A hurricane brings people together to do good. Neighbors help neighbors. Neighbors talk to neighbors to see if they are ok. Neighbors share their food and supplies that another neighbor needs.

The animals and bugs are confused. They seek shelter to any dry place they can find. They swim to find their homes. An armadillo found shelter snuggled up against a neighbor's door eating her plants. Tofu wore his raincoat in case he needed to leave in a hurry.

The schools were closed. Children were creative in their play after the hurricane. They went fishing and discovered some eels and tiny fish in their nets. They also played with remote control cars in the water.

The water dries up. The branches and dirt are cleared. Those who sought shelter return to see their homes. The tow trucks remove the stranded cars. The flowers bloom. The rainbow forms. A new day is coming.

This is what happened in my grandma's neighborhood. It was her first hurricane in Florida. People said Ian was different from all others. Ian came and Ian left. Now the sun shines brighter in grandma's neighborhood.

Hurricanes affect everyone differently. Many in Florida were left without their homes and belongings. Rescue and recovery efforts are happening round the clock to change destruction to reconstruction. We all need to help. Find out what you can do to help.

https://voadflorida.wpengine.com/

Pat Goldys

Pat Goldys was born in Baltimore, Maryland and lived there for 63 years. She loves steamed crabs, carmel creams and snowballs. She moved to Florida to be near her granddaughter, Mila.

Pat continues to write stories about real events, as well as the make believe. Kids like fiction and nonfiction. She writes stories that kids like to read and parents and grandparents can read to their children.

If you choose to read, please leave a review as I'd love to read your thoughts!